LOVE BETWEEN THE LINES

MAX COPPA

Love Between the Lines
©Copyright, Max Coppa, April 30 2014

All rights reserved. No part of this publication may be reproduced, distributed, or transmitted in any form or by any means, including photocopying, recording, or other electronic or mechanical methods, without the prior written permission of the publisher, except in the case of brief quotations embodied in critical reviews and certain other noncommercial uses permitted by copyright law. For permission requests, write to the publisher, addressed "Attention: Permissions Coordinator," at the address below.

inSpirit Publishing
28 Hickson Circuit
Harrington Park NSW 2014
www.inspiritpublishing.net

ISBN 9780987452740
Printed in the Australia
First Printing, 2014

Cover design by Nicola McIntosh
website: www.nicolamcintosh.com
Palmistry artwork by Nicolle Poll
Contact: www.facebook.com/artworkbyNicolle

LOVE BETWEEN THE LINES

How the secret art of palmistry can help you
to better understand your
sex life and personal relationships

MAX COPPA

Dedication

I dedicate this book to my beautiful wife Amanda who has shown me more about life than any other person I know. She expresses her love to me and our children every day and asks for nothing in return. She has taught me to be patient, forgiving and to always look on the bright side of life.

Contents

Foreword	6
Introduction	10
Chapter 1 - The Hands Have It	13
Chapter 2 - All Fingers & Thumbs	35
Chapter 3 - The Mounts	63
Chapter 4 - Love Those Lines	72
Princess Diana	93
Karen - Case Study 1	96
Jan - Case Study 2	98
Catherine - Case Study 3	100

FOREWORD

This book has been written primarily to help you better understand your sex life and personal relationships. Unbeknownst to most people, your hands reveal volumes about your personality; likes, dislikes and importantly the way you love and how you share that love with others. This book will show how the lines on your palms, finger lengths, hand shapes and more, reveal your most intimate secrets and how they can help you to get the very best out of yourself and your love life.

WHAT IS PALMISTRY?

Palmistry is more commonly known as "palm reading" and is based upon the idea that it is possible to tell about a person's character, past and future simply by observing the marks on a person's palm. This is a form of divination. The "handbook" of palmistry was written by a man named Cheiro, a famous Seer during the 1920s and 30s. His real name was Leic de Hamong, aka Louis Hamon, and he argued that there were two different facets to palmistry, one dealing with the general shape of the hand and another dealing with the lines and markings which are found on the hand. According to Cheiro, merely examining the lines and markings results in a superficial or incomplete reading. Instead, the entire hand must be taken into account, thus making the subject much more complicated than it first appeared.

Where Does Palmistry Come From?

The science of palmistry is almost as old as love itself. Among the ancient Chaldeans, Assyrians, Egyptians and Hebrews, the study of palmistry was widely respected and used for purposes of divination and fortune-telling, but today it is used to read and counsel. In India and China, palmistry can trace its roots back as far as 3000 BC. Legend has it that Aristotle, who also knew and practiced the art, discovered a palmistry tome written in golden letters that he presented as a gift to Alexander the Great. Plato, another great philosopher, also held palmistry in high esteem.

Even the Bible makes reference to the art of palm reading. "He sealth up the hand of every man that all men may know his work" (Job 37:7). Despite this biblical reference, palmistry was frowned upon by the

Roman Catholic Church during the Middle Ages and was, along with many other occult arts, suppressed, although it still enjoyed an underground popularity and was practiced by gypsy fortune tellers.

During the nineteenth century in Europe, and especially in France, the art of palmistry reemerged with the publication of the works of Carus, D'Arpentingny and Desbarrolles. At this time there were two different palm reading subdivisions: Cheirology, the study of manual formations and peculiarities and Cheiromancy, the art of divination of the lines, marks and shapes of the hands. Today these two subdivisions have merged under the umbrella of palmistry.

How does palmistry work?

Since the turn of the century, palmistry has been regarded as a branch of fortune telling, yet on closer inspection it involves much more than simple predictions for the future. After studying palmistry, Carl Jung (the founder of analytical psychology) is quoted as saying; "hand whose shape and function are so intimately connected with the psyche might provide revealing and therefore interpretable expression of psychological peculiarity, that is, of human character".

I see palmistry a little differently to most people in that I believe it represents a balance of both the physical and spiritual worlds. When we are able to balance these worlds, we can live in harmony and express love naturally. Finding the right life partner or true friend comes easily, then, as we are balanced ourselves, giving out the right signals to attract those who will exert the most beneficial influence in our lives.

During my long career as a palmist, I have also come to the understanding that although we are masters of our own destiny, at times we need a little direction. The old adage of 'know thyself' is very relevant to palmistry for it is in the palms of our own hands that we will find clues as to how and in which direction we should steer the course of our life.

With a little practice, you'll be able to recognise instantly the features indicating different character traits – both positive and negative – saving yourself a lot of time and heartache in the dating game! If you're already in a relationship, a palmistry analysis of your own and your partners hands can help you both understand each other much better. As you learn the basic principles of palmistry described here, try its lessons with an open heart. You'll be amazed at how the lines on the hand can show you how to attract and keep love in your own life. Remember the lines on your hands are changing all of your life, the dominant hand more so than the non-dominant hand. Love can change them for good or bad.

INTRODUCTION

LOVE AND SEXUALITY, IT'S ALL IN THE HANDS

"What about my love life?" During my career of more than 35 years as a practicing palmist, I've found that this, probably more than any other, is the most commonly asked question. "*Will I find my perfect partner?*" is another very common one.

From the hardest bitten cynic through to the most dreamy idealist, we all share one common interest. Love. We all need love, the crown of human emotion. Through relationships we are able to express this need – both giving and receiving love and thus growing as individuals. Whatever type of love we may experience during the course of our lives, be it the romantic kind, the love we hold for family, friends and children or a non-physical, spiritual meeting of souls, love helps us to transcend ourselves. It is essential for both our spiritual development and our psychological well-being. The hand and the lines of the palm can reveal the capacity we have to love, how we are to be loved in return and most importantly, when we are most likely to find true happiness.

The aim of this book is to provide you with the tools to enable you to find the answers to these questions and more. Both for yourself and for others. Once you know what to look for, your lovers hands can tell you exactly what sort of person they really are. When you look at your lovers hands, are they strong with flexible thumbs, or are they perhaps soft and square shaped with longish fingers? Are the fingers widely spaced or set together fairly closely? What about the texture of the skin on the hand?

Once you learn the secret language of the hands, you'll be able to interpret at a glance the tell-tale signs like these that may reveal your perfect match in love. Did you know, for example, that a long thumb indicates that your lover is more likely to be faithful but more strong-willed than their shorter-thumbed companions? Or if you are interested in his bed-time prowess, look no further than the size and shape of his Mount of Venus and Mount of Mars (the pad of flesh found at the root of the thumb) – the bigger it is, the more passionate the lover! Should you want a lover who is discreet and good at keeping secrets, beware of those with very short middle fingers. This indicates a degree of immaturity, low morals and a tendency to blab their (and your) innermost thoughts!

Remember that its best, at first, to learn how to read your own palms and then go on to compare them with those of your present or potential partner. This way you'll maximize the chance of getting it right and will confidently recognise shared compatibility clues.

CHAPTER 1

THE HANDS HAVE IT!

Throughout the ages, humans have looked at their palms to provide answers almost in the way that today we might look at a roadmap for direction. In a sense, your palm is actually a blueprint for your life's journey. Understanding this blueprint enables you to access information not only about future trends but also about a whole range of 'here' and 'now' issues such as relationships, health, work, money and travel. Looking at the palm, first take note of the size and shape of the hands, the mounts, the lines on the mounts and the lines interlacing the palm. For right-handed people, the left hand reflects inbred characteristics and the right hand acquired characteristics. The opposite is true for left-handed people. Each mount signifies a certain personality trait with the four most important lines representing life, intelligence, the heart and personal fortune. Also important are the size and shape of the fingers and the fingertips.

Your hands show you the spiritual and physical directions that lie before you. Although you ultimately determine your own destiny, at times we all need a little glimpse of the road ahead in order to give our lives meaning and purpose. Past events and conditions have conspired to make you what you are today while the present holds the seeds of opportunity for shaping the future. Palmistry can help illuminate past weaknesses or strengths, the knowledge of which can empower you to steer a wiser course for that future. At first trying to read a palm may appear to be a little overwhelming. The key is to take it step by step and remember to have fun while you're learning – and soon you'll be well on the way to understanding the secrets of your own and your lover's palm.

One of the most important things to remember when you begin to analyse anyone's hands (including those of your partner) is to always read both hands. Most people have a dominant hand, meaning they are either right-handed or left-handed and the dominant and non-dominant hands have different meanings.

The non-dominant or passive hand; (the one you don't use to write with) shows your basic personality, natural aptitudes, characteristics, past and current events and inner life, as well as your innate potential. It is the reflection of the innermost you.

The dominant hand; (the one you do use to write with) shows how your personality has changed or is likely to develop. It indicates future events as well as what you are doing with your life right now.

Very often, the hands reveal marked differences between our innate potential and the degree to which it is being fulfilled.

Size

The first thing you'll notice about your own or your lover's hands is the size. Most people have roughly the same sized hands, although women's hands are marginally smaller, in general, than those of men. From time to time though, you'll no doubt encounter people whose hand size is at the extreme of both ends of the scale.

Small Hands: Contrary to what you might expect, a person whose hands are small is intensely interested in the grand scheme of things. They see life on a big scale. Fiercely ambitious with visions of grandeur when it comes to lifestyle, they like big houses, big cars and always have an eye on the main chance. As lovers though, they can be nitpickers who may drive you crazy with their nagging. They tend to like drama and are drawn to the erotic and purely physical side of sex. Often guided by pure intuition, they tend to be more emotional than mental. In love, they are risk-takers who love living through the senses.

Large Hands: These are the hands of an attentive lover. If these are your hands, you look at life in great detail, particularly when it comes to relationships. You're the sort who will ponder long and hard before making a commitment, but once you've run the idea through that analytical computer brain of yours and the data has come up looking good, you're very user-friendly – and loyal. Your powers of concentration and memory are legendary, so any partner should be forewarned against trying to pull the wool over your eyes with stories about exactly where they were and with whom on the night of the 14th eight months ago!

Thickness

Thickness of the hand is also a very good indicator of exactly how much sexual energy we have at our disposal. To check the hand for thickness, view it from the side. Take note, though, that other factors, such as the size of the Mount of Venus and the depth of the lines (more on this later), can modify what a thickness reading can tell you. Remember the rule in palmistry is to take everything in the hand into account.

Thin Hands: A person with thin hands is often lacking in true warmth of the heart, a quality vital to a really deep and lasting relationship. This is especially true if the hand is hard as well as thin, indicating stubbornness, inflexibility, reserve and a somewhat secretive, calculating approach. They may not always be 100 per cent truthful, and they can also be real misers when it comes to spending money in a relationship.

Thick Hands: Here we find the complete opposite to be true. A thick hand reveals an abundance of warm energy and sensuality. If the hand is thick and soft as well, they'll love sex and especially food, and may have difficulty maintaining a balanced weight. A thick hand that is also hard and inflexible usually indicates someone who is sexually aggressive as well as emotionally demanding, thinking mostly about self-gratification. This person would prove very difficult to live with, as basically there is too much take and not enough give.

Extremely Thick Hands: Beware of the person with this sort of hand. Everything is done to excess, including eating and drinking. If you don't want to end up with a potbellied partner in later years, avoid becoming involved with this hand type.

Medium Thickness: Of course between these extremes is a hand of medium thickness, which reveals a fairly easy-going sort of person with a healthy and balanced outlook on life and romance. Sex is seen as a normal and pleasurable part of living. No big dramas here!

The Basic Hand Shape

There are four basic hand shapes, plus the occasional mixed shape, but remember every person is unique. Naturally you wouldn't expect to find a hand that looked exactly like one of these illustrations – more often than not you'll find a mixture of one or more types. Nevertheless the diagrams do provide a basic guide to recognising an overall shape and what it means.

The Square Hand – The Capable One: This is one of the most common hand types that you'll find. Look for a palm that forms a square between the wrist and the base of the fingers. Often, the fingers themselves are broad, squarish with large-

THE HANDS HAVE IT!

The Square Hand

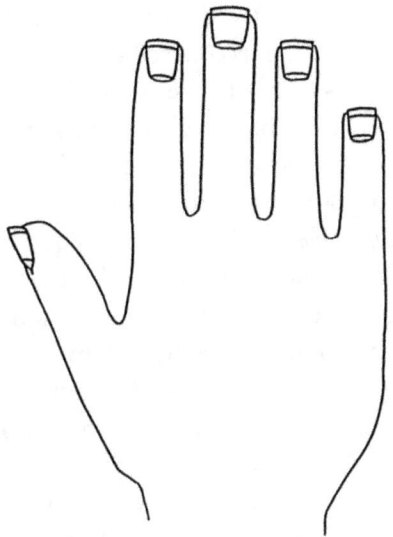

My Notes:

_____

_____

_____

_____

_____

_____

_____

tipped fingers. If your lover has a hand like this, count yourself lucky as they're no slouch in the love game. They believe in taking time to make love well and often. You can recognise the partners of the square hand types – they're the ones who are usually smiling contentedly. But don't expect never-ending bedroom pyrotechnics. The square hand is also intensely interested in practical matters. *"What are we having for dinner tonight?"* is a more frequently asked question than *"Do you really love me?"* Commonsense and reason do tend to overshadow emotion in these people, and they prefer a steady, systematic approach to love and relationships. (A word of advice: if your man has a square hand, don't have the TV near the bed when the footy is on!).

Square hand types are always interested in the bottom line: their bosses happily refer to them as 'results-oriented'. Once in love, however, they are equally as professional at handing in a good performance in the relationship as they are at work. If you're looking for someone who offers dependability, stability and patience through thick and thin, don't go past the square hand.

The Spatulate Hand - The Love Machine: This type runs on love. They need it to exist like others need air. You can recognize the spatulate shaped hand by the tendency of the fingers to flatten out at

THE HANDS HAVE IT!

The Spatulate Hand

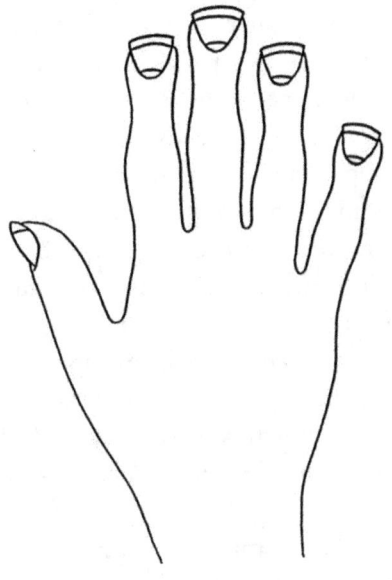

My Notes:
_____
_____
_____
_____
_____
_____
_____

the ends, forming a fan shape, often accompanied by slightly knotted finger joints. The palm will be broad and strong in appearance. If you're lucky enough to have a partner with this type of hand, you can expect them to be innovative, highly sexed and adventurous in lovemaking. They love excitement and can be charming company but woe betide anyone who thinks a spatulate hand is going to be theirs and theirs alone!

If the hand feels very soft as well as being spatula shaped, they'll want to pursue the pleasures of the flesh even more. They're the type who, for example, may want you to join them in group sex, or other types of kinky indulgences. Sometimes these people are so immersed in activities of this kind, that other responsibilities – like earning a living – may take a poor second.

If you're a woman looking for long-term commitment from a spatulate man, forget it! Unfortunately, these types are born flirts, the kind who enjoy the thrill of love and romance but are rarely there for the long term. However there's no need to despair quite yet – other factors in the hand may modify this tendency. On the plus side, spatula types do rate highly as enthusiastic lovers with plenty of stamina. They're usually sporty types who enjoy plenty of fresh air and exercise – preferably outdoor lovemaking!

The Conic Hand - The Creative One: Those with conic shaped hands are much more receptive, intuitive and romantic that the two previous types. Look for hands that have long palms with tapering fingers that begin full at the base of the finger and end in slight points. Highly creative, conic hands enjoy excitement, spontaneity and open discussion in a relationship. They will very quickly tire of routine, particularly in lovemaking. In bed, you'll need to be as versatile and innovative as they are. Although not having quite so much energy and stamina as those with spatula or square hands, conic hands will more than make up for this by being able to instantly recognise your mood and tune into it.

Mr Conic is a sensitive and imaginative lover who adores food, beautiful surroundings and intelligent conversation – a true sophisticate who's not afraid of treating a woman with romantic tenderness and old world courtesy. If, however, the hand is also bland and fat, the sensuous nature is especially exaggerated. It's the hand of a big eater, maybe even with a tendency towards alcoholism (this in conjunction with other lines will confirm this). This type is also into lots of sex, although you may find that as you both grow older together, their libido will rapidly decline. They'll tire easily and won't be able to keep up with you sexually.

The Conic Hand

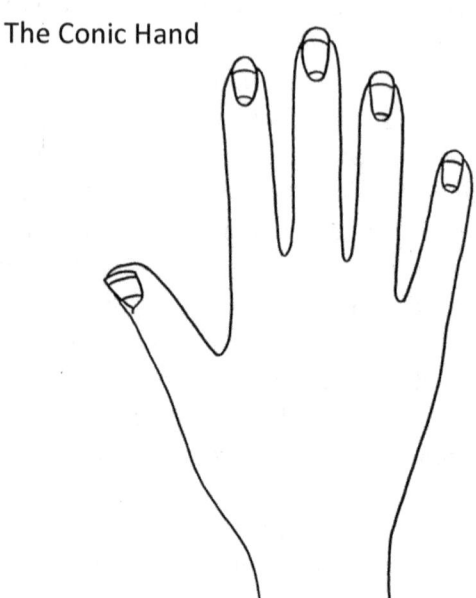

My Notes:

_____
_____
_____
_____
_____
_____
_____

Inconsistency and instability are the major problems with the conic hand; they're the kind who say they love you one day and are gone the next. If, however, your partners conic hand is also firm and strong, there is a better chance there'll be more commitment and that the relationship will last.

The Psychic Hand - The Dreamer: You won't see too many people with this type of hands as they are relatively rare. This kind of hand is beautiful to look at – they're the ones you see in classical sculpture, or in paintings by old masters. Also known as the 'pointed hand', both the palm and the fingers are narrow and elongated, with a delicate and sensitive appearance. This is the hand of the dreamer who is motivated by deep intuition and 'psychic flashes'. In the everyday world, however, psychic hands tend to be hopelessly out of their depth and will need you to mother him or her if any sort of relationship can endure.

With a tendency to place his partner on a pedestal, Mr Psychic's idea of romance is of the impossibly chivalrous kind. He'll write you long, beautiful and flowery love letters. In fact, a relationship with this man often works best when it is conducted from afar as generally it is simply too fragile to stand the rigours of daily reality. Should you decide to team up anyway, you'll definitely need to be the strong and steady one who can help 'ground' this type in the real world,

LOVE BETWEEN THE LINES

The Psychic Hand

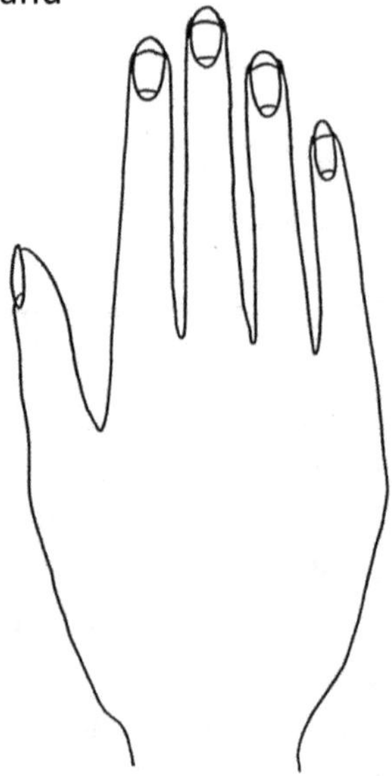

My Notes:

_____
_____
_____
_____
_____
_____
_____

offering them the stability they lack. Expect to be the partner who takes out the garbage in this relationship!

The Mixed Hand - The All-Rounder: If you've got a lover whose hands are a mixture of two or more of the shapes mentioned, look at the most dominant feature in the hand and read each aspect separately. Read the basic shape first, then look at the fingers, mounts and lines as well as the size, skin texture and flexibility of the hand itself. Generally speaking, though, lovers whose hands combine several key features are usually adaptable, clever and enthusiastic. They're the types who can usually get along with a wide range of possible partners. Just as long as you share their enthusiasm for a latest hobby or craze, you won't have any trouble keeping them loyal to you. They like plenty of fun in a relationship. They also like some time on their own, so that when you do get together again everything's hotter than ever!

LOVE BETWEEN THE LINES

The Mixed Hand

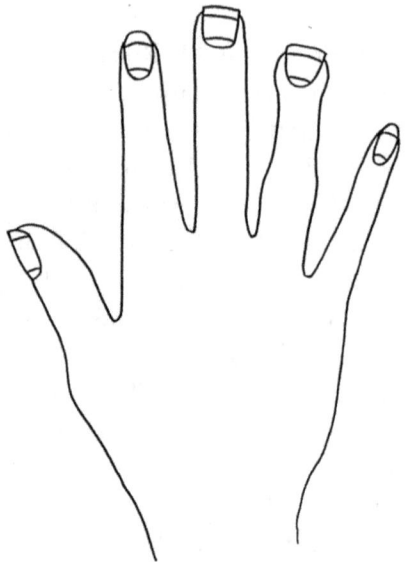

My Notes:

_____
_____
_____
_____
_____
_____
_____

Firmness

Firmness of the hand is yet another important tool to use in palmistry analysis. Take your partners hand between yours and feel how firm it is. Does it feel strong yet pliant, or is it very soft? Perhaps it's somewhere in between. Defining how firm your partner's hand feels is a great way to 'instantly' get to the bottom of whether or not you are compatible. For example, a relationship between two people with very soft hands could be a fairly wishy-washy affair with little or no sexual fire. If, however, you are the one with the soft hands, choose a mate whose palms have more resilience and bounce that yours and whose skin is firm. That way you'll ensure that there will be a certain drive or energy to the relationship.

Soft Hands: Generally speaking, the softer the hand the gentler the nature. However, sometimes this type could infuriate you by being a little too easygoing – to the point of being lazy. They're happy just to sit back and let things take care of themselves. There's no point trying to enjoy an argument with a soft-handed person as they usually give in too easily.

Elastic Hands: Elastic hands are the ones that tend to spring back under pressure. They are the hands of someone who is full of vitality and who enjoys inventing and creating. They'll respond readily to any new ideas you may put their way. They're flexible and ready to try anything once, including adventurous lovemaking positions. This type is very receptive to visual stimuli so make sure your packaging looks good!

Firm Hands: These are the mark of a person who has great strength of character. They pride themselves on being physically fit. They also know their own mind and won't give in too easily to pressure of any kind, however subtle it may be. Possessing a certain charisma, this type tends to have others looking to them for leadership.

Hard Hands: Hard hands are ones that don't yield under pressure, and neither does the person they belong to. This type tends to dominate in a relationship and can be very bossy. Often very set in their ways, hard-handed people are notorious for 'holding in' energy, betraying a lack of willingness to trust. For a relationship, this can spell disaster.

Skin Texture

The next step is to look at what sort of skin texture the hand has. There are three types; smooth and fine, hard or coarse and medium.

Smooth, fine skin: Hands with this type of skin

indicate a sensitive type, an idealist who loves all things romantic. A heightened sense of fantasy means that they'll adore you whispering sweet (or naughty) nothings into their ear as you make love!

Hard or coarse skin: A very revealing characteristic in the hand, this skin type is generally only found on men, although a few women do possess it as well. A man with coarse or hard skin is usually a very physical type with lots of energy. He'll love outdoor sports of any kind and is what you would call a real 'mans' man. In love, he believes that 'what you see is what you get', and he has no time or patience for the more subtle aspects of romance. This may mean that often he won't be receptive enough to your sexual needs, especially if you are a woman who happens to have a fine, thin hand. Again, remember the rule; look at other factors in the palm which may modify this tendency.

Medium skin: The ideal type of skin texture in a man or woman, it demonstrates a healthy and balanced outlook on life and relationships. The person with medium skin doesn't 'stress out' unnecessarily when problems arise. They are open to your needs and wants without making doormats of themselves in the process.

COLOUR

The next thing to look at is the overall colour of the palm. Is it a healthy colour or is it pale? Is it of one colour or does there seem to be a certain patchiness? If it has a nice colour, then you've probably got a good-natured, cheerful type on your hands – generally an optimist who tries to make a relationship work. If the palms appear somewhat too pale, energy levels are probably low. There may even be a tendency to anaemia, so if your partner's palms are very pale for any length of time, it's probably a good idea for them to have a health check.

Speckled palms: Are a sign that the person needs some time alone to release pent-up emotions. Palms like these can be identified by small white spots near the surface of the palm.

Reddish palms: Indicate an excess of energy, aggression, a volatile temper and a tendency towards self indulgence. It can also be an early warning sign that heart conditions may be a problem later in life.

FLEXIBILITY

As you might expect, someone with a flexible hand has a greater capacity to adapt to new ideas and situations than someone with a more rigid hand. In a relationship, a man or woman with a flexible hand would be caring, sharing and generous. Those with extremely flexible hands – hands which can bend back from the wrist to a 90 degree angle or more – are also known for their unpredictable behavior, spontaneity and generosity. The inflexible hand indicates a rigid, stubborn personality, someone who feels ill at ease with new ideas or situations. They are not good socially, so if you're planning a party, give them something to occupy themselves with so they don't feel obliged to mingle.

In Conclusion

By now you should have a basic idea of what to begin looking for in a palm. Don't worry too much if it sounds confusing – practice makes perfect, especially in palmistry. The more hands you read, the more confident you'll feel and the better palmist you'll become. Take it one step at a time and soon you'll see the different parts of the jigsaw taking shape. Once you have assessed the basic features of the hand as described in this chapter, the next step is to take a look at some even more revealing indicators of personality: the fingers.

Flexibility

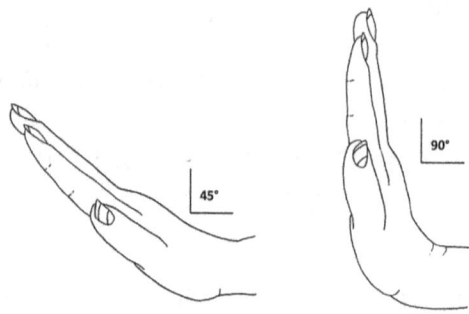

My Notes:

_____
_____
_____
_____
_____
_____
_____

CHAPTER 2

ALL FINGERS AND THUMBS

When studying your lover's palms, you need to look at finger length and width, thickness, flexibility, and any usual characteristics. The fingers will give you information on sexual personality, and whether someone is timid or forthcoming when expressing their sexual feelings. This area of the hand will also give you the information on passion levels and how someone's innermost mind works. It is important to study each finger both by itself as well as in relation to the rest of the hand. To get the whole picture, you must take note of the relationship of each finger to the other. You will also need to keep an eye out for injuries or cuts – they may confuse your reading.

Length and width

Finger length is a good place to start your study. Finger length is judged in relation to the palm, using the middle finger as a guide. Measure the middle finger with a ruler, then measure the palm from the start of the wrists to the base of the middle finger. An average middle finger length is one which measures roughly three-quarters of the length of the palm. Fingers which measure less than this are considered to the 'short', while fingers longer than this are termed 'long'.

Now for their meanings:

Short fingers: Those with short fingers generally tend to be heady, impetuous types who love drama and rely on instincts rather than reason. Intuitive, impulsive and impatient, they usually go straight to the heart of any problem, especially within the context of a relationship and often want to rush in and make love on the first date. They tend to dislike poring over too much detail and prefer to look at the bigger picture. They often have great management potential.

Long fingers: Opposite qualities hold true for this finger type. This person is somewhat of a perfectionist who loves to analyse and probe. They adore detail and are patient and thorough. In relationships these are the fingers of someone who usually needs to make sure that the setting or timing is exactly right before they make that first romantic move. They are loyal, whether as a friend or as a lover, but, if hurt, they can harbor grudges for a long time.

Thick fingers: The thicker or fleshier the fingers are, the more sensual the person's nature. They enjoy luxury, rich food and of course, lots of sex.

Thin fingers: A person with thin or bony fingers is more or less disinterested in the material world. They are a more intellectual type who prefers to stay at home and read a highbrow book than get down and 'boogie' with you!

Knotty fingers: Knotty fingers which are not caused by an arthritic condition reveal an analytical mind and a passion for logic and detail. As people with knotty fingers find it difficult to express their feelings to others, communication problems can arise in relationships with them.

Flexibility

Flexibility of the fingers, like flexibility of the hand itself, is an important clue in determining character. Ideally, the tips of the fingers should arch gently backwards when stretched out. This denotes an ability to adapt to new ideas and situations. Those with extremely flexible fingers – fingers which can bend back from the top of the palm to a 90 degree angle or more – are also known for their unpredictable behavior, spontaneity and generosity.

This is the paw of a real party animal who enjoys being outrageous. Should you have a partner with stiff or inflexible fingers, you may find that they are sexually conservative. They may, for example, want to make love only when the lights are off, or only at set times during the week. A rigid personality is indicated here.

Phalanges

These are the areas between the finger joints and indicates a person's outlook on and interests in life. This quality is a good one to take note of in terms of long term relationships and compatibility. All the fingers are divided into three parts or phalanges and the comparative length of these sections vary from finger to finger. The bottom phalange – the one that joins the finger to the palm – is slightly longer than the other two phalanges which are usually equal to each other in length.

Top Phalange: This represents the mental order of

Finger Flexibility

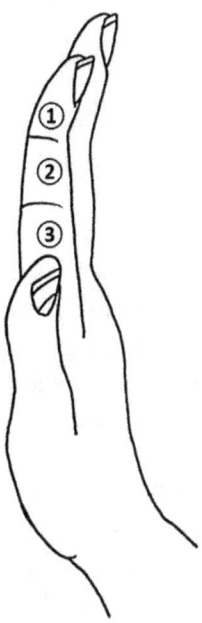

My Notes:
_____
_____
_____
_____
_____
_____
_____

the person. If this is the longest of the phalanges on the finger it indicates the intellectual and spiritual approach to life.

Middle Phalange: Indicates the practical order of the person. If this is the longest it reflects a practical and capable nature.

Bottom Phalange: Highlights the material order, one's love of the material aspects of life. If this phalange is long and thick then the person is prone to have strong money-making skills and needs to surround themselves with material possessions.

Fingertip Shape

To determine the fingertip shape, place the hand palm-side up and focus on just the tips of the fingers. Their shape can tell you what motivates their owner and how they see their direction in life. As for the hand itself, there are five main types of fingertips:

Conic Fingertips: People with conic fingertips are highly imaginative, poetic and creative. This shape indicates a penchant for the unusual. Pointed tips are the mark of a daydreamer whose sexuality needs to be ignited by fantasy.

Square Fingertips: Usually the possessor of

this fingertip type is honest and reliable. They are somewhat conservative in approach and have a great sense of duty and an affinity with tradition. Not liking a great deal of variety in their lives, they are happiest in safe and secure surroundings. This is a lover who won't make mad passionate love to you in crazy places, but if you can bake an apple pie like their mother used to make then you have a partner for life!

Spatulate Fingertips: Spatulate fingertips generally indicate a lover with drive and energy. If you are the object of their affection, they will pursue relentlessly until they have conquered and won. Once in a relationship, they will not take kindly to any obstacles barring them from full sexual intimacy. In fact a 'no' may actually spur them on!

Round Fingertips: Round fingertips are very indicative of a 'people person'. These types are social animals who enjoy being at the centre of very large gatherings. Expect to share this partner with several friends as their love of variety and concern for others is a key to their personality – they always like to be available if someone needs their shoulder to cry on. Should this kind of popularity sometimes threaten you, remember that they are also flexible and sensitive enough to listen to and accommodate your emotional needs as well.

Fingertip Shape

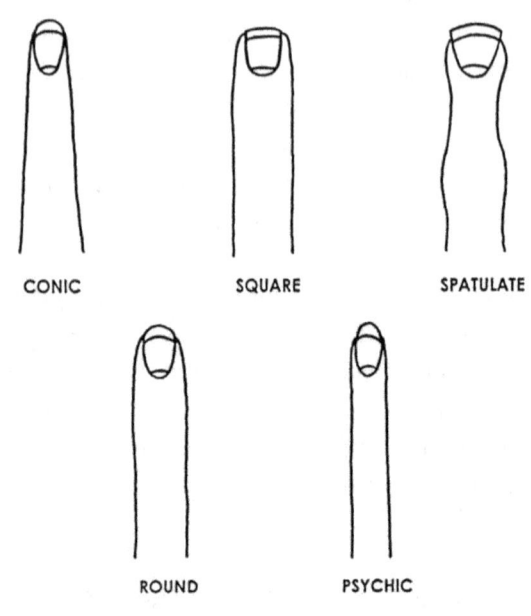

My Notes:

_____
_____
_____
_____
_____
_____
_____

Psychic Fingertips: Indicate quiet people with a romantic nature. These people are sensitive to the needs of others and are easily hurt. These types need to be wined and dined constantly. Love letters, poetry, classical music and old movies are the keys to opening their hearts to love.

Finger Names

Each finger of the hand is named after one of the Roman gods, and was linked to Astrology. These names symbolise different sorts of energy. The index or first finger is called the Jupiter Finger, the middle or second finger is called the Saturn Finger, the ring or third finger is called the Apollo Finger and the little finger is called the Mercury Finger. The thumb does not have a special name in palmistry.

Firstly, get your partner to open their hand completely with the fingers held slightly apart. Next, see if the fingers lean towards one in particular. If they do, then we can say that this particular finger is the dominant one in the hand, providing you with an instant 'key' to their character.

Now let's take a look at the significance of each finger in turn and see what they can tell us about personality.

The Jupiter Finger: Also known as the first or index finger, this is the strongest finger and expresses the degree of authority or leadership a person possesses. This 'pointer' finger is associated with ambition and the drive to succeed in life. Ideally, it should be the same length as the Apollo finger and shorter than the Saturn finger, indicating a person who is a considerate and thoughtful lover – someone who is also a natural leader without being too pushy.

A Jupiter finger that is longer than the Apollo finger, however, indicates an overbearing personality, which does not auger well for a relationship. This type has a large ego and will want to own you. They are however, extremely astute in business where they generally rise to executive positions.

On the other hand, if the Jupiter finger is shorter than the Apollo finger, poor self esteem is apparent. A short Jupiter finger betrays a lack of self-confidence. This is a shy type who needs a strong partner to balance them, however they must at all costs avoid being too eager to please. In a relationship, this type of partner will always ask your opinion before making a decision.

A thin Jupiter finger shows a need for a stronger lover who initiates sex. This will bring out the best in this type.

A thick Jupiter finger indicates a type that is headstrong and determined. In a relationship this person needs spoiling and likes plenty of sex. Be aware that this type may want to dominate.

If the Jupiter finger bends towards Saturn, watch out for tendency towards possessiveness, jealousy and an overly materialistic tendency. If the Jupiter finger bends towards the thumb (the will), this person will be outgoing and ambitious and want to succeed.

The Saturn Finger: The second or middle finger will tell you how cautious your lover is. It denotes propriety, responsibility and introspection. Usually the longest finger on the hand, the Saturn finger reassures the conscience of a person and their values in life.

A Saturn finger that is of average length, that is, just a little longer than the first and third fingers, is the mark of a well balanced person who has a healthy attitude to life and love.

A long Saturn finger in a partner shows a lover who is over-cautious. They may take ages before they are willing to truly commit themselves in a relationship. However, once they have weighed up the pros and cons and have come to a positive decision, they will do their utmost to make the relationship succeed.

A short Saturn finger shows a carefree nature with an unwillingness to be tied down to routine of any sort. They are good diplomats, often to the point of being a little too glib. This type enjoys travelling and experiencing everything that life has to offer. That includes relationships with a wide variety of

Finger Names

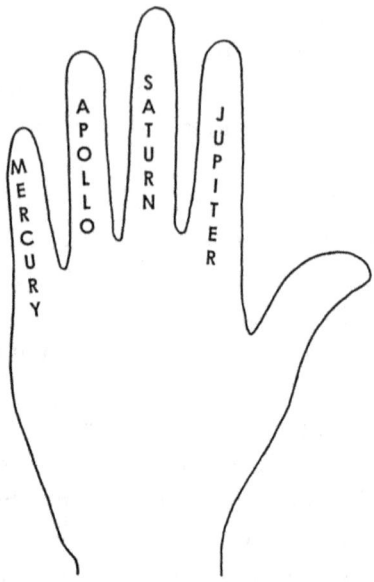

My Notes:

_____
_____
_____
_____
_____
_____
_____

partners. Before they are ready for commitment in a relationship, they will need to have sown their wild oats.

A very short Saturn finger is a warning to be careful. Avoid telling them too much about your private affairs as, more than likely, you'll hear the juicy details being discussed on the grapevine the very next day. This type can't help being a blabbermouth! These types can be totally unreliable and can be lacking in moral standards. When the chips are down this person cannot be counted on.

A thin Saturn finger shows a tendency to be self-critical. This type of person may have no personal goals and needs to be led in relation to love matters.

A thick Saturn finger indicates a person who is serious and inhibited. This is reflected in their lovemaking which can border on the very conservative. A sense of humor is lacking in this type. In a relationship, this person may need to be taught how to lighten up and laugh.

When the Saturn finger curves towards Jupiter, the personality is an outgoing one. They always like to be surrounded by a large circle of friends, even in a relationship.

When the Saturn finger curves towards Apollo, there is a need to be alone. A partner with this finger type needs lots of personal space.

When the Saturn finger curves sharply towards

Apollo there is a strong tendency towards melancholy and depression.

The Apollo Finger: The third or ring finger rules creativity, love of art and music. The Apollo finger is the finger of romance. This is the finger that shows you what capacity your lover has for living life to the full, enjoying its finer offerings.

An Apollo finger of average length (one that is approximately nine-tenths the length of the middle finger) indicates a balanced outlook and a person who is creatively productive in their field, which is usually related to the arts. In a relationship they are consummate practitioners of the art of give-and-take.

A long Apollo finger shows a strong intellect. Long and straight Apollo fingers are found on many artists, actors and performers of any kind. In love, they crave physical contact and have considerable powers of seduction. They love admiration and may tend to flit from one relationship to another seeking a perfect, idealised kind of relationship. Naturally enthusiastic, these people tend to attract others with their warmth and radiance.

A short Apollo finger is the mark of someone who is a little reluctant to believe firmly in themselves. However, with encouragement from a loving partner, this type can gradually be persuaded to come out of their shell. Although not as artistic as the long Apollo finger type, they do nevertheless make creative and enthusiastic lovers.

A thick Apollo finger emphasizes the qualities of a long Apollo finger – a quick and sharp intellect, extroverted and idealistic. This type craves attention.

A thin Apollo finger shows a weakness in character and is a little unimaginative in love play.

An Apollo finger that leans towards Mercury signifies a lover who adores bright conversation and new ideas, they are very creative and inventive in all areas – especially lovemaking. As they are great animal lovers, make sure you pay attention to their favourite pet if you want to impress them.

An Apollo finger that leans towards Saturn is the sign of a gambler, this is emphasized when the Jupiter and Apollo finger are the same. There is also a tendency to overestimate others which often results in disillusion.

The Mercury Finger: The fourth or little finger is named after the god Mercury famous in myth as the messenger with winged feet. The Mercury finger expresses a person's intuitive understanding of their environment and their ability to adapt quickly to changing circumstances. It is the finger of communication and self-expression.

A long Mercury finger (one that is more than seven-tenths the length of the middle finger) shows someone who has great powers of persuasion and communication. In relationships, this person will always tell you exactly what they think. These people definitely have the 'gift of the gab' and make great salespeople or politicians. They must, however, guard against the temptation to become overly slick in manner.

A short Mercury finger denotes bluntness of speech, the mark of someone who is sometimes too truthful to the point where they can hurt or offend others. If your partner has this type of little finger, they will probably choose their words carefully and not verbalise too much. They have an aura of lovable vulnerability that is almost childlike. Sadly, there is an indication here of difficulty in establishing relationships. There may also be sexual problems present. A Mercury finger that is both short and sharply turned towards the Apollo finger denotes an element of untrustworthiness in relationships.

A thin Mercury finger with a flexible tip shows musical talent and an appreciation for harmonious surroundings.

A thick Mercury finger is a warning sign to others that this is an argumentative person. Whatever the issue, they will voice their opinion loud and strong and will not give in until they have persuaded you that they alone are right.

A Mercury finger that curves towards Apollo

signifies an astute, diplomatic nature. This lover will whisper sweet nothings in your ear to make you smile. A definite type to turn your head. In a relationship, you can trust your innermost secrets to this person.

A Mercury finger that curves towards the hands outer edge is the mark of a daredevil – someone who has loads of energy and who is always in high spirits. They express themselves differently and may be a little kinky in lovemaking.

Rings on Your Fingers: Rings on the fingers of the hand can also tell a lot about a person and how they express themselves. People make statements with rings, and I believe rings are good for us, they are bands that bind our love, and an expression of that love and joy for another person that we have committed ourselves to.

A ring on the Jupiter or index finger of the dominant hand shows a drive to succeed in business and spiritual matters. It may frighten men when a woman wears a ring on the index finger. This becomes less intimidating when worn on the non-dominant hand, but a desire to achieve is still evident. The ring on the Jupiter finger goes back to medieval times when kings, church leaders and prominent men of the community wore big sealing rings on this finger highlighting power and control.

A ring on the Saturn or middle finger indicates

personal achievements and beliefs. Women are wearing rings here now as their goals are much more important to them these days. Never wear a tight ring as it restricts.

Wearing a ring on the Apollo finger shows talent and success as well as acknowledging marriage. The arts, creative ability and wealth are also represented. Too many rings on this finger shows a person may be ostentatious and possibly a bit of a gambler.

A ring on the Mercury finger will help with love matters and helps communication with partners. So if you want love to work or you have problems in this area, wear a ring on the little finger. Most relationships break down because we fail to communicate. A fine appreciation of music, writing and the arts is also indicated.

Wearing a ring on the thumb strengthens the power of the will. A ring here represents a sense of empowerment and personal strength. In Pagan days wedding rings were worn on the thumb.

Gold or silver rings are both good conductors of energy, the choice is a personal one. I have left out stones. Birth stones will enhance the energy of the finger it is worn on.

Finger Spacing

Checking the spaces between the fingers is a fun way to get instant clues about yourself or your partner.

Let their hand rest on the table, palm up and flattened slightly and see where the largest spaces are between the fingers. Fingers that are generally held fairly close together indicate a person who is cautious and hardworking with a fairly serious point of view. Wider spaces indicate that the person is feeling confident in their ability to rise to the challenges before them. The spacing between individual fingers is also very telling.

Widest space between thumb and first finger: This is the sign of someone who is generous to a fault. If you're in a relationship with this type of person and operate a shared bank account, watch their tendency to flash that credit card around a little too freely! On the positive side, they are open-minded, kind and tolerant, and won't be the sort of lover who is always checking up on where you've been.

Widest space between first and middle fingers: For a partner in love, you can't go past this type for maintaining a cool head at all times. They are very reasonable and will listen to you explaining why you need that new CD player (or whatever) without interjecting or being obstructive. However, if your partner has this hand and is also committed to another relationship, it will be very difficult for them to find the necessary gumption to sever that tie to be with you only.

LOVE BETWEEN THE LINES

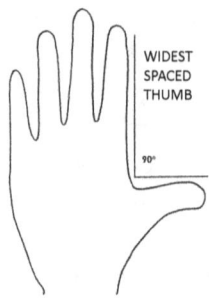

WIDEST SPACED THUMB

90°

WIDE SPACE BETWEEN FIRST AND THIRD FINGER

My Notes:
___
___
___
___
___
___
___

Widest space between middle and third fingers:
This indicates a bohemian at heart who loves laughing in the face of convention. Expect surprise treats and mystery trips away together, as this kind of person really knows how to put the spice into a relationship.

Widest space between the third and fourth fingers:
This is the sign of a very independent type. Very little will deter this person from following a particular course of action once they have made a decision. As a partner in love, this can work to your advantage – once they have chosen you, that's it. You can rely on their undying loyalty. This type loves to talk.

Thumbs up!

The thumb is very different in both shape and function to the rest of the fingers. As it is opposable to the rest of the hand, it has played a significant role in the evolution of humans as creative beings who can manipulate their surroundings. Since they could grasp and hold objects, our early ancestors had a distinct advantage over the rest of the animal world, hence the thumb has set us apart from most other species. For this reason, palmists regard the thumb as an indicator of will. It can reveal just how much determination and intellect you have, how strong your ego is and how sexually energetic you are.

A normal thumb length will reach to the middle

LOVE BETWEEN THE LINES

WIDE SPACE BETWEEN MIDDLE AND THIRD FINGER

WIDE SPACE BETWEEN THIRD AND FOURTH FINGER

My Notes:

of the first phalange of the first finger. This person is great company and makes a good mediator.

A long thumb that reaches beyond the lowest joint of the first finger indicates a person with a forceful personality and an enormous amount of sexual energy. Fortunately, these people are very faithful in love, although they can be very domineering and demanding of their partner. They like to think that they are the centre of your universe.

A short thumb rises to the first phalange crease, the joint between the palm and the first finger. This thumb length indicates a weak-willed person who must take care not to become a pushover in a relationship. They are big softies and have a weak spot for flattery. Easily led, they can quickly become the target of more predatory rivals in love who may try to steal them away from you. They are hopeless flirts.

A flexible thumb has an angle of sixty degrees or more between their thumb and the side of their first finger, you can expect the unexpected! Disliking routine, they inject stacks of romance into a relationship with surprise gestures and impulsive treats. They will avoid like the plague anything that smacks of being in a rut. This makes for an interesting relationship which you just won't be able to take for granted. It may, however, become a little too hard on the nerves for someone who prefers a more steady pace.

A stiff thumb is one that can't make a right angle with the side of the first finger. It signifies someone who is very rigid-minded and set in their ways. Overly cautious and sometimes withdrawn, they have an almost Victorian attitude to sexuality and are embarrassed by any frank discussion on the matter. Of course, other aspects in the hand may modify this tendency. They are, however, almost religiously faithful to their chose mate.

A thick, jutting thumb indicates a very strong character, someone who has no problem at all in imposing their will on others.

A 'waisted' thumb is one which narrows in the middle. It is the mark of a very logical mind. A lover with this type of thumb will also be articulate and can smooth-talk their way out of tricky situations.

Thumbs with 'clubbed' or bulbous ends is also called the 'murderers thumb', it does not necessarily signify homicidal tendencies. It does, however, mean that this person tends to harbour deep resentment, which frequently results in sudden outbursts of temper and even violence. Fortunately, only a small proportion of people possess this type of thumb.

Thumbs with thin ends show a person who is emotionally quite timid. A lover with this type of thumb will look to you for leadership. If you prefer a partner who is the decisive type, this sort of person

ALL FINGERS AND THUMBS

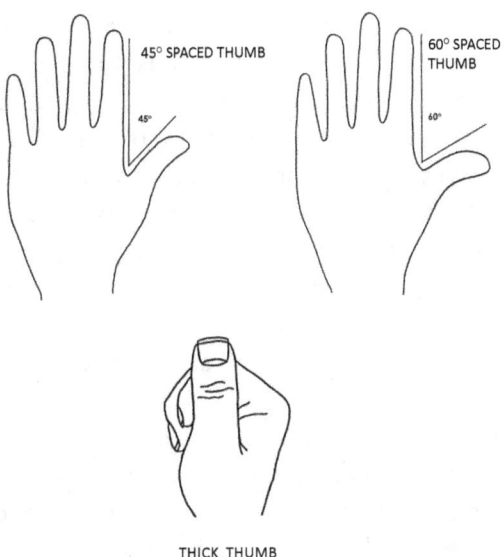

THICK THUMB

My Notes:
_____
_____
_____
_____
_____
_____
_____

may annoy you with their over-eagerness to please.

Thumbs with squarish ends belong to a no-nonsense type. This person's approach to a relationship will be practical and rational. They may, for instance, plan their lovemaking with you.

Thumbs with spatulate ends reveal someone who runs on instinct. They are highly-strung types who tend to be impatient and become agitated very easily. Although having a dynamic personality, a partner with this type of thumb will be very scattered.

Thumbs with pointed ends show a person who is intuitively quick to understand any mood changes in their partner. Their impulsive nature however, means that they can't focus their energy for long enough to solve any problem requiring persistence.

The Nails

The shape, size and length of your lover's nails can also help you to better understand their temperament. The length of the nail is measured from the cuticle to the beginning of the white part of the nail.

Long, broad and slightly rounded nails indicate open-mindedness, generosity and a willingness to cooperate with others.

Long narrow nails show a tendency towards suspicion and selfishness. If the hand contains no other modifying indicators, this person will be calculating and shrewd. In relationships, this type of

ALL FINGERS AND THUMBS

WAISTED THUMB

CLUBBED END THUMB

My Notes:
_____
_____
_____
_____
_____
_____
_____

lover usually thinks only of themselves and how to use others to further their aims.

Short nails reveal an individual who is prone to vent scathing criticism on their partner or friend should they not meet their expectations. Rarely do they give praise.

Naturally reddish nails expose a hot lover! Their passion is strong and they express this physically – and often.

Naturally bluish nails indicates a person who has a rather cold temperament. In love, they are very slow to express their innermost feelings, often to the point where they are mistakenly believed to be disinterested in their partner.

In Conclusion

We've seen how the fingers can be an extremely good indicator of a person's temperament. Next we will look at the mounts and in particular one of the most fascinating and revealing passion zones; the Mount of Venus.

CHAPTER 3

THE MOUNTS

The padded contours under the fingers are referred to as mounts in palmistry. Any good hand-reading analysis should take these, together with the lines on the palm, as very good indicators of personality. The size of the mounts in your own or your lovers hands provide a key to character type.

Higher mounts indicate a sensuous energy and someone who has an active outgoing personality. High mounts indicate the dominance of personality type.

Low or soft mounts mean that the qualities of

that particular mount are either not being fulfilled or are totally lacking.

There are several mounts which denote seven different types of personality. As for the fingers, each mount has a name which is symbolic of the energy it represents. For example, the Jupiter mount indicates leadership qualities, the mount of Saturn shows beliefs and personal goals and the mount of Apollo shows creativity. Communication is represented by the mount of Mercury, dreaming and inner vision by the mount of Luna and courage is symbolised by the mount of Mars. Finally, the mount which is most important in any study of love and relationships is of course, the mount of Venus.

Venus: Mount of Passion

More than any other mount on the palm, the mount of Venus will reveal exactly how your mate rates in the passion stakes. Ideally, this mount should measure roughly one-third of the palm's surface. It should be neither too hard nor too soft but resilient to the touch.

If your partner has a prominent mount of Venus, they'll be loving, caring and generous. If you're a lucky person whose partner's palm displays this characteristic, expect to be pampered and adored. Your lover will give you loads of attention and will really listen to you.

THE MOUNTS

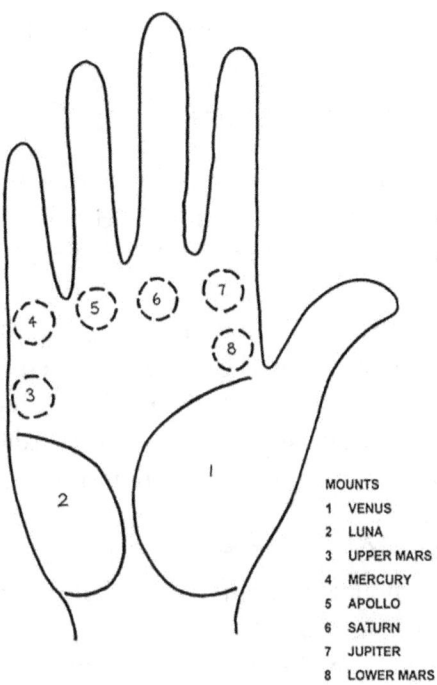

MOUNTS
1. VENUS
2. LUNA
3. UPPER MARS
4. MERCURY
5. APOLLO
6. SATURN
7. JUPITER
8. LOWER MARS

My Notes:

_____
_____
_____
_____
_____
_____
_____

Should your partner have a palm whose mount of Venus is full and / or wide this means that your affair will be intensely physical, with lots of hugs and kisses.

Someone with a less developed mount of Venus is usually a person who is more reserved and cautious.

A flat mount of Venus indicates a cold emotional nature.

An interesting observation regarding this fascinating mount; during my years of studying palms, I have noticed that if one of my clients experiences a strong love affair, very often this can actually cause an increase in the size of their mount of Venus.

Jupiter: Mount of Ambition

The mount of Jupiter symbolises drive, ego or desire for achievement.

A high, firm Jupiter mount is the mark of the born achiever – a leader who gets things done with the utmost professionalism and style in both personal and business matters. They are self-assured and generally others tend to look to them for guidance.

A soft, flat Jupiter mount shows a much more hesitant type of personality but one who is, nevertheless, a good listener and friend. They much prefer someone else to take the lead.

Saturn: Mount of Judgment

The God Saturn was traditionally seen as a stern taskmaster, signifying judgment and limitation. As the Saturn finger (and mount) is at the centre of the hand, it represents balance. The Saturn mount is associated with conservatism and analysis.

A high, firm Saturn mount indicates that its owner has great powers of concentration and loves detail. Should your mate possess this type of mount, be prepared for sharp (and sometimes cruel) analytical comments about you, your friends and even the way you dress. This type has an eye for detail and a maddening knack of remembering the most trivial things – especially ones you'd rather forget!

A soft, flat Saturn mount indicates a more free-wheeling type, someone who isn't afraid to explore life and all its possibilities.

Apollo: Mount of Creativity

A high, firm mount of Apollo is a mark of great creativity. A partner with this type of mount is great at creating a cosy, artistic love nest for the two of you. They have an in-built sense of flair, and they use shapes and colour in a highly imaginative way. Their decorative sense also extends to the way they dress. If you need sound fashion advice, go shopping for clothes with this type.

A soft, flat Apollo mount shows an enjoyment of creativity but to a lesser extent. This sort would prefer to watch others create, and may need encouragement to help them bring out their hidden artistic abilities.

Mercury: Mount of Communication

Like the winged messenger its named after, the mount of Mercury is associated with quickness of mind and shrewd observation.

A high, firm Mercury mount usually has a powerful grasp of language. This is the mark of the persuasive sales person. There is a need, however, to guard against appearing too glib, especially when it comes to relationships.

A soft, flat Apollo mount shows a person who needs to make themselves very clear when communicating as they are all too readily misunderstood and their motives misinterpreted. They must rely more on their very well developed intuitive abilities. This person needs encouragement to express their inner feelings. You will find that this type prefers to write love letters rather than declaring their love face to face.

Mars: Mount of Courage

The Mars mount is divided into Upper Mars (located under the heart line) and Lower Mars (located inside the life line). Both of these mounts signify determination and courage in the face of adversity.

THE MOUNTS

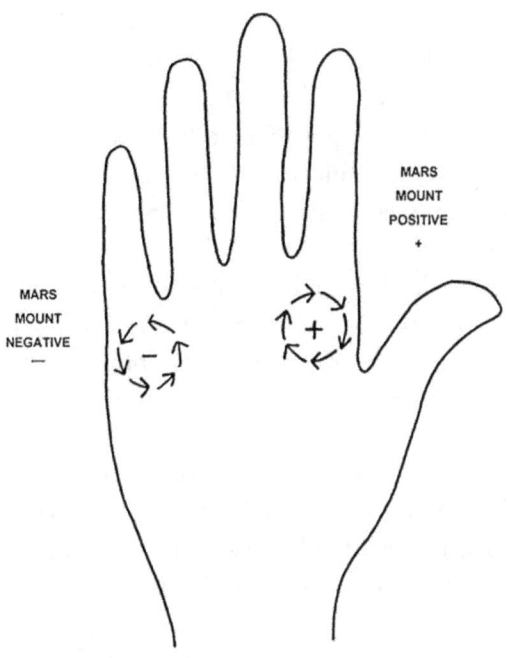

My Notes:

_____
_____
_____
_____
_____
_____
_____

The energy of the upper mount is more passive (negative), while that of the lower mount is active and assertive (positive).

A high, firm Upper Mars indicates someone who is courageous and full of confidence – definitely the leader in any relationship. This person can often be very stubborn.

A soft, flat Upper Mars indicates someone who may need a little encouragement from you to let their true courage shine through. Sometimes they are a little timid in relationships, but they are definitely not wimpy!

A high, firm Lower Mars indicates a real powerhouse of energy and drive. There is no way this person's will won't win! This type can be aggressive and bad tempered. The path of love won't always be smooth.

A soft, flat Lower Mars shows someone who is more steady and persistent in achieving their goals rather than roller-coasting their way. Obstacles spur them on.

Luna: Mount of Mystery

The mount of Luna is found at the lower base under the little finger where the wrist joins the palm. It is associated with mystery, inner vision and dreaming.

A high, firm Luna mount is a good indication that you're in for romance with a capital 'R'. This person is the sort who suggests surprise trips to mystery destinations or romantic strolls in the moonlight. For them, life is one big adventure.

A soft, flat Luna mount is the mark of a more pragmatic lover. This person is much more likely to make sure that you're both wearing comfortable shoes before suggesting that romantic walk.

Finally, when looking at the mounts, don't forget to consider them as part of the overall palmistry evaluation; so that you get the whole picture. Also, remember that people with opposite love mounts can attract, more often than not achieving a mutually satisfactory and enduring relationship.

CHAPTER 4

LOVE THOSE LINES!

Coming to grips with the lines on the palm may appear a bit daunting at first, but if you take it slowly, step-by-step, you'll quickly get the hang of it. The first thing to understand is that every line, from the longest to the shortest, has a beginning and an end. It is the variation along the path of a line that reveals its meaning.

Perhaps the most important lines are the Life, Head and Heart Lines. Also extremely important are the Fate, Sun and Mercury lines. Of course, there are many other meaningful small lines and marks on the hand but to start off with, a study of these fist six

LOVE THOSE LINES!

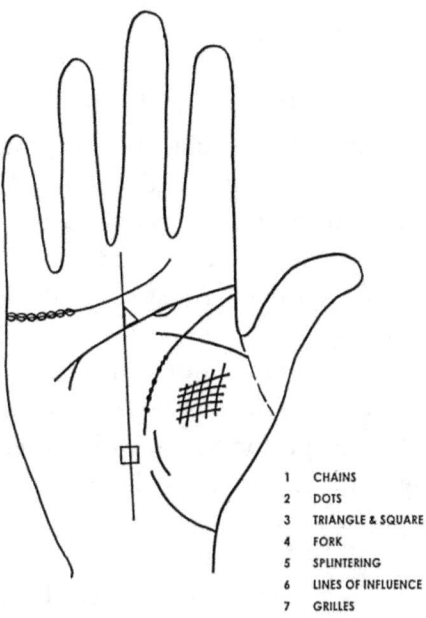

1. CHAINS
2. DOTS
3. TRIANGLE & SQUARE
4. FORK
5. SPLINTERING
6. LINES OF INFLUENCE
7. GRILLES

My Notes:

_____
_____
_____
_____
_____
_____
_____

lines will give you ample information about yourself and your partner.

Quality and Quantity

Ideally, lines should be clear and well defined, with an even depth and width. Very deep lines indicate an excess of energy while broad, shallow lines show a tendency towards dissipation of energy. Generally speaking, the stronger the line the stronger the influence.

The number of lines on the hand is also important. An abundance of lines reveals a nervous disposition, the type of person who is easily upset while few lines suggest that someone has little sensitivity and is more the physical type.

- Lines of influence are small lines which run parallel to, or cross vertical lines. They indicate times of important events such as marriage, children or even loss of relatives.

- Splintered or split lines indicate a new period in someone's life. Although this means the strength of the line is weakened, it may simply be a sign of change rather than a negative sign.

- Islands do mean that the line on which they appear is weakened, to the extent that its main energy is scattered.

- Grilles also reveal scattered energies – for example, if your partner has one on their mount of Venus, they are very likely to be sexually overindulgent and can also indicate negative sexual problems or inhibitions.

- Chains indicate a lengthy period of weakened energy in the line where they appear.

- A dot indicates a setback of either an emotional or physical nature.

- A fork depending on its location, means either a weakening of the line, or balance and adaptability.

- Squares and triangles are signs of protection and can often repair a broken line.

The Life Line

Another question I frequently hear as a palmist (besides "How's my love life?") is "How long will I live?" Unfortunately things are not quite as cut and dried as clients expect. Even if it were possible to tell exactly when you would die, ethics prevent a good palmist from doing so. The life line is not meant to reveal when one will die but rather describes the way

LOVE BETWEEN THE LINES

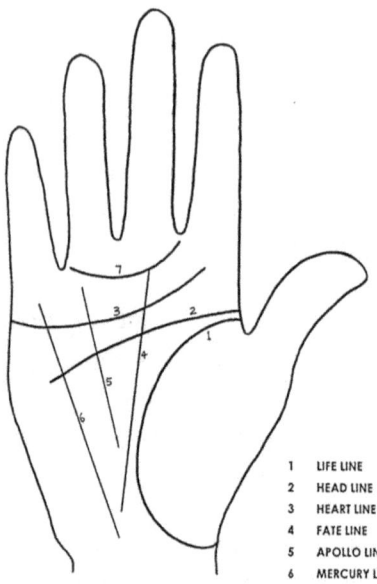

1. LIFE LINE
2. HEAD LINE
3. HEART LINE
4. FATE LINE
5. APOLLO LINE
6. MERCURY LINE
7. GIRDLE VENUS

My Notes:
_____
_____
_____
_____
_____
_____
_____

one lives. It can tell you about your physical heredity and your chances for good health in the future. It can reveal your early childhood, circumstances, your family and your chances of travel and success. It can also be used to indicate the time at which important events occurred or will occur in the future.

Where to find the Life Line

This is the one which encircles the thumb (see Diagram). It begins at the outside edge of the hand, just under the index finger and travels to the base of the palm. The best type of life line for sexual relationships is one which curves around the mount of Venus in a generous arc, suggesting a strong and healthy interest in sex. Should your partner's life line cut through the mount of Venus, diminishing its size, there could be a problem with sexual relations. A life line that moves downward towards the mount of Luna, under the little finger is the mark of someone who likes a variety of sexual partners, has a vivid imagination, fantasises or can be very restless.

The Head Line

Also called the line of the mind, this line reveals intelligence and mental capacity as well as psychological disposition. It doesn't actually indicate how smart someone is, but rather it shows the strength of their determination and the way they think. The head line can also reveal any mental illness or nervous disposition which may affect sexual expression.

Where to find the Head Line

This line begins near the life line under the index finger, ending under the ring finger. If your partner or loved one has a head line that is both long and straight, they are likely to be practical when it comes to relationships. If you yearn for imaginative bedroom techniques however, you may find they lack a little fire.

A head line sloping sharply towards the Luna mount indicates that they can be very imaginative in bed. Fantasy is important in their lovemaking. A sloping head line can also indicate a tendency towards depression if romantic advances are rejected. Islands in the head line signify a lack of consistency in relationships. A fork in the head line shows a talent for writing and counseling.

The Heart Line

The heart line is probably the most important line to assess if you are looking to palmistry for answers to questions about love and relationships. This line is truly an emotional barometer as well as revealing the way in which we express our sexuality. In this sense, it is a window to our passion. Generally speaking, the longer the line the more intense is the passion.

Where to find the Heart Line

Beginning at the outside edge of the hand under the little finger, the heart line runs across the top of the hand, either finishing under the index or middle fingers or somewhere between them.

Length

If your lover has a very long heart line (one that extends from the outside edge of the hand and ends beyond the Jupiter mount), you've got a red hot lover on your hands! This is a mark of great intensity of emotion and indicates an all or nothing attitude to relationships. Although they will lavish love and gifts on you, they will expect the utmost loyalty and devotion in return as they are idealistic about love – don't forget the flowers or chocolates.

If the heart line ends on the Jupiter mount this is the sign of someone who lives for love. This type is considerate and affectionate in love, so there is a good chance of a lasting partnership. A short heart line ending beneath the mount of Saturn and branching up the Saturn mount suggests a more sensual than romantic approach to love. This is reinforced if the mount of Venus is well developed. This type of partner is not always patient or considerate. A line ending between Jupiter and Saturn shows that this person is well balanced in their outlook on love.

Curvature

If the heart line is curved, this is the sign of the 'touchy-feely' type, the sort who really does wear their heart on their sleeve. Open and enthusiastic by nature, they are great motivators for those around them. If your partner has this type of line, they will be warm, caring and sexually assertive. A curved heart line which sweeps generously across the palm predicts happiness in love.

If the heart line is straight, the opposite to the above holds true. This is a person who is reserved and detached by nature, although sometimes their aloofness makes them appear even more desirable. In love, although they seem cool on the surface, their feelings actually run deep. Knowing this, they take their time to commit, not wishing to risk showing their inner emotional vulnerability.

It is important to remember that other factors in the hand come into play in the overall evaluation of personality. For example, as we have seen, a straight heart line does tend to cool down passion. If the rest of the hand indicates a sensual nature, the person will have strong physical love urges but will be detached emotionally.

The Girdle of Venus

This line is very rarely seen in its entirety. Only pieces of the line appear. The girdle of Venus line is effectively a secondary version of the heart line. Although, not a feature in everyone's hands, when present it is a very special indication of high sensitivity and an artistic temperament. Should your partner have a girdle of Venus, they will love to indulge in fantasy and sexual imagery, especially if the line is broken. While this line certainly helps to enhance emotional and sexual responses, if it reaches the Mercury finger, it could be a sign of someone with a moody disposition, leading to problems.

The Fate Line

Also known as Saturn's line, the fate line deals with character and career. It describes our responses to life's opportunities and challenges and the choices we make.

Where to find the Fate Line

This line runs vertically from near the centre of the bottom of the hand to the top of the palm under the middle finger. If you look at your own or your partner's hands, you will see that the fate line is not simply one line but is made up of two or more lines falling in roughly the same vertical track under the Saturn mount. This is logical since very few people today have the same career or relationship throughout the whole course of their lives.

Depth

A deep fate line shows where there has been or will be great success. This marks the most significant phases of our lives. A shallow fate line which appears to be barely there shows periods of uncertainty and indecision. To the trained eye, breaks in the line can mean divorce.

Timing

The fate line can indicate at what time important life changes occurred or will occur, and the mark of a really professional palmist is the ability to interpret this timing accurately. The time on the fate line begins at the bottom of the hand, with the first 40 years of your life shown between the starting point and the head line. The next ten years are located in between the head and heart lines, while ages 50 to 80 are found at the relatively small space between the heart line and the top of the palm.

The Apollo Line

The Apollo line is also known as the sun line, and with good reason. The qualities associated with this line are warmth, spontaneity, cheerfulness, creativity and money. If you are fortunate enough to have a partner with a good Apollo line, you will love basking in the glow of their usually sunny nature. They will have a certain charisma which draws admirers like moths to the flame. If you can handle the competition, well and good!

Where to find the Apollo Line

Look for a vertical line located under the third or ring finger. A long Apollo line is the trademark of someone who is the life of the party. This type thrives on being the centre of attention. A short Apollo line indicates someone who is more of a quiet achiever, but who still manages to shine in their own way, especially in any creative endeavors, usually later in life. Judgment of character is not good for this type and they will be constantly let down by others. A straight Apollo line signifies success and recognition. A wavy Apollo line indicates success that is spasmodic. A deep Apollo line is the mark of a winner, someone who knows the sweet smell of success. A shallow Apollo line still has the promise of great things but is a quiet achiever.

The Mercury Line

Although small in comparison to the other major lines, the Mercury line is an important indicator of how successfully a person can communicate and how much business sense they possess.

Where to find the Mercury Line

This is the diagonal line that begins at the bottom

of the hand and continues up the hand, ending under the little finger.

A long Mercury line indicates a partner whose business acumen is without equal. Usually at the top of the corporate ladder or at the helm of their own business, they enjoy being movers and shakers. This type is sexually active and communicate their feelings well, both verbally and sexually.

A short Mercury line indicates someone who has the potential to rise to the top in business, but who must take things carefully and learn from others first. Watch this person's health for stress as these people tend to hold back their feelings.

A straight Mercury line in a partner's hand shows that they are nobody's fool when it comes to getting the best deal. This goes for personal relationships too!

A wavy Mercury line is the sign of someone who is a little hesitant at times to take the plunge. They may need business advice and personal reassurance from you before they feel confident enough to handle office politics. This type can be scattered and unfocussed when trying to express their love verbally. Physically they are more demonstrative.

A deep Mercury line indicates prosperity as well as good health. A shallow Mercury line shows you need to watch your health. If it is broken into little dashes, this is a sign of nervous tension, often related

LOVE THOSE LINES!

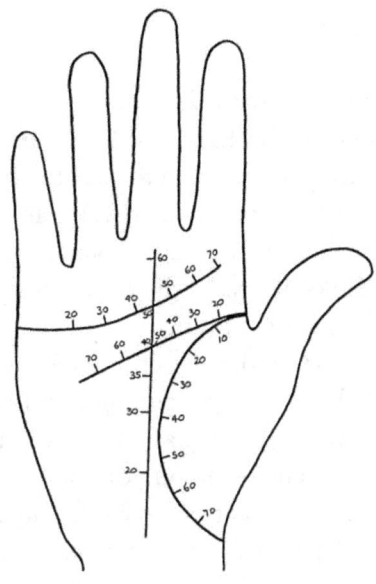

My Notes:

_____
_____
_____
_____
_____
_____
_____

to work pressures.

Timing on the Hands

Timing on the hands is quite easy to read, and with practice you can learn to read the highs and lows of one's path. You need to refer to the following diagram to help you along. Make a note of breaks, changes, forks and with the time lines you can work out times of certain events.

Hold your hand, palm up and look at your life line. It starts below the Jupiter mount and travels around the Venus mount to the base of the mount, where the wrist begins. The beginning of the time line starts at 0. Forty years sits halfway down the line, opposite the centre of the thumb. Seventy years sits at the base of the bottom of the thumb. When you have found these points, divide them into equal parts as shown in the diagram. Each division point represents 10 years.

The head line starts from the same place as the life line and travels across the hand, the 40 year mark sits at the centre of the line, midway across the palm. Divide this line into equal parts. Again, each division point represents 10 years.

The heart line starts under the Mercury finger and travels towards the mount of Jupiter. Halve and divide this line into equal parts, moving towards the Jupiter Finger.

The fate line is a bit different and a bit more

complicated to read. Start at the base of the wrist and move up towards the Saturn finger. The 40 year point sits on the intersection of the head line, 50 years is on the intersection of the heart line and above this lies the following years. You need to refer to the diagram to see the breakdown of the years on the line.

The Mercury line is measured in a manner similar to the head line, as it starts at the base of the wrist near the life line and usually ends on the head line under the Mercury mount. Divide the line in half, this point is 40 years and divide the line into equal spaces, each point representing 10 years. The final point under the Mercury mount is 80 years.

Keep in mind that each hand is different, so the spacing must be equally proportioned into 10 year periods. It is then divided again, to get the exact time/age of the person when events take place in their life.

The Simian Line

This fairly unusual line is found when both the head and heart lines combine to form one line cutting horizontally across the upper palm. A Simian type lover is one who is always intense in relationships, often becoming overwhelmed by their own emotions. These people need an understanding partner who can help balance them, and who is not easily offended by their often extreme behavior. They run hot and cold without explanation and are most often changeable

LOVE BETWEEN THE LINES

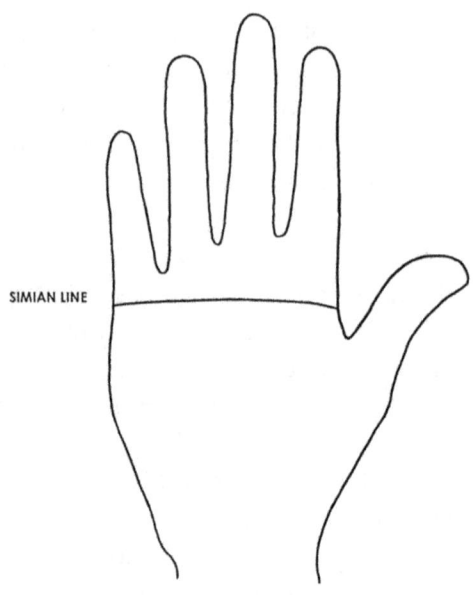

My Notes:

___
___
___
___
___
___
___

and moody. A Simian type lover can be unpredictably violent or even sexually aggressive, yet they are generally bright and intelligent. However, it is always wise to examine the hand as a whole before making an evaluation.

Relationship Lines

In the past, palmists referred to relationship lines as 'marriage lines'. Of course, in today's society this has widened in meaning to include relationships which don't necessarily end in marriage, but which are equally rewarding to the partners involved.

Where to find Relationship Lines

Ask your partner to gently close their hand. Between the outside edge and immediately under the base of the little finger to the heart line, you will see small horizontal lines. These are the relationship lines. It is important to understand that these lines, like other small lines, are able to change in appearance. For example, when a relationship is about to begin, they will deepen. Similarly, they will fade as the union dissolves or sexual desire grows weaker. Deep relationship lines indicate a correspondingly deep commitment to a relationship. An absence of relationship lines does not necessarily mean that there will be no relationships. If your partner has none of these lines, it shows that they have a casual attitude

LOVE BETWEEN THE LINES

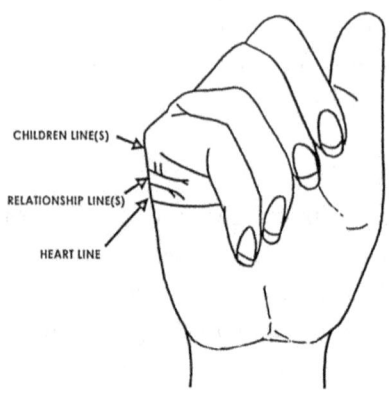

My Notes:

_____
_____
_____
_____
_____
_____
_____

to romance and are not committing themselves to the relationship. More than one relationship line does not always signal more than one relationship. If multiple lines are found on the hand of someone who is happily married or content in a partnership, it could simply indicate a growing happiness with that same person. If, however, there is more than one relationship line found on the hand of someone who is newly single or just divorced, this is a sign that potential relationships will soon be formed.

Children Lines

Contrary to popular belief, children lines don't always represent the number of children you or your partner have or will have. Instead, they are signs showing that it is possible to have children in your life and the potential number of children you could have.

Where to find the Children Lines

These are very fine vertical lines found immediately above the relationship lines, and you may need to use a magnifying glass to see which lines stand out more clearly. Read from the outer edge of the palm for the first born and then continue inwards for subsequent children. Deep children lines usually mean biological children, although they may also represent stepchildren. Boys are generally indicated by long, deep lines. Short, narrow and fine children lines indicate girls. Two small lines rising from the same point are a sign of twins. A total lack of children lines corresponds with problems in conceiving a child.

When looking at the children lines it must be remembered that, as with other lines, your own free will needs to be taken into account. For example, should you see on your own or your partner's palm one outstanding child line, you must also ask yourself if in fact you want a child. You must first decide and then leave the rest to fate.

Princess Diana

THE PEOPLE'S PRINCESS

Many years ago I was fortunate to be able to see prints of Princess Diana's palms and they revealed a lot about her. From the powerful Fate line that rose in the Mount of Luna and ran right up to the Mount of Jupiter (under the index finger). This meant that she would have great success and influence over people. However, the other side of her true nature was also shown. A chained Heart line revealed her struggles in love and her Life line showed childhood issues had tested her.

The most interesting line on her hand was a Girdle of Venus. However, it was different to most, in that it ran in to the relationship lines on the Mount of Mercury. This meant that she believed in fidelity, thought love would last forever and that one day the Princess would be the wife of a King. When she wasn't, she was devastated. Diana's relationship lines showed she had affairs because of her emotional wounds (a few of them) and disappointments in love.

Interestingly, Diana did have a small break in her Life line at the time of her death. It was a very telling and dangerous sign on the palm and indicated a sudden death.

I see Diana as a person who gave much more than she took, and was a lonely person who just wanted love. So, as you can see, love (and the journey of love) can make or break us. Learn to read the signs and make your journey of love a whole lot easier and much more rewarding. The palms never lie!

PRINCESS DIANA

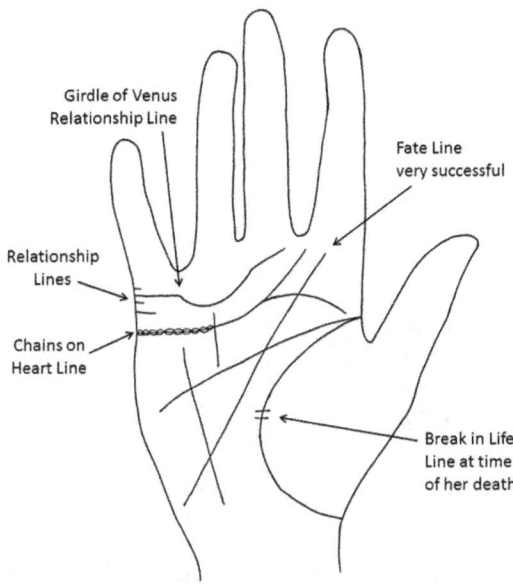

My Notes:

Karen

CASE STUDY 1

Karen has a well-defined Life Line both in terms of length and quality of life. She is driven and has a strong Fate Line (career line) which shows she has two paths of career. A clear Head Line shows she has a quick and intelligent mind. A lovely Heart Line ending between the Jupiter (index finger) and Saturn (middle finger) fingers is the right place for true romantics and lovers. The tip of her Thumb bends back revealing her giving and loving nature.

Karen has endured tests in life and love, but will always look on the bright and positive side. Her short Mercury Finger (pinkie finger) and two Relationship Lines shows that love and relationships won't always

LOVE BETWEEN THE LINES

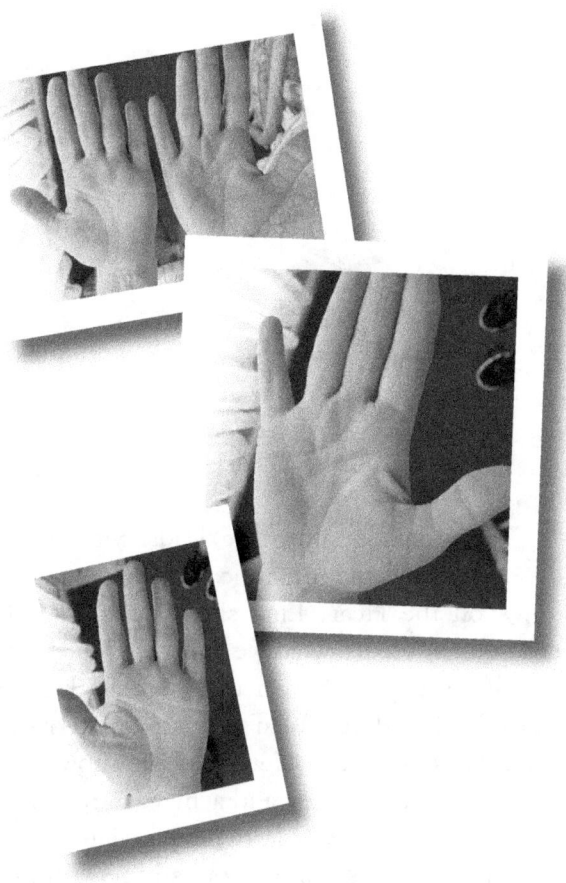

be easy, but do we ever stop trying for love?

Jan

CASE STUDY 2

Jan's hands show she leads with the heart and is a true romantic. The bumps and dips on the Heart Line shows love has had its challenges, but that's what we are on the earthly plane to rectify through experience. A broken Head Line reveals this has affected Jan's thinking patterns which she has since rectified. Her Fate Line shows she has a strong drive to succeed and achieve in her life. She has natural teaching and leadership qualities with her work and directions standing out strongly for her.

Jan is very spiritual and intuitive with wonderful creative flare that is calling right now. People have tried to control her in the past, however Jan knows she is the master of her own ship. The fractured

Life and Head Line coupled with a chained Family Ring on the Thumb point to early childhood stress (family) which has only made Jan stronger and more determined.

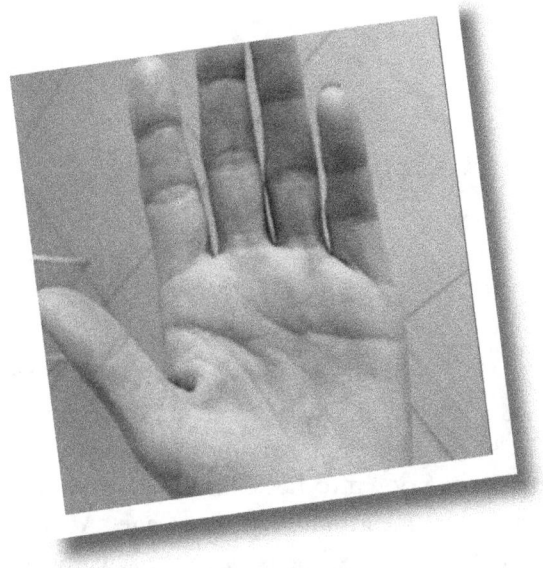

Jan likes nice things around her and must always do work she loves. There are lots of new journey's for her now which she will enjoy.

Catherine

CASE STUDY 3

Catherine's hands show a troubled childhood with many ups and downs. This is shown by the flared Heart Line which turns down to her childhood at the beginning of the Life Line around 8 years of age. As strong and as talented as she is, she is also very sensitive which is shown by the fineness of the skin ridging. A straight and long Saturn Finger (middle finger) shows she is honest with strong values and beliefs. A slight kink in the Mercury Finger (little finger) shows Catherine expresses herself differently to others. The red mark on her Mount of Venus shows relationship troubles are coming to an end. Stigmata Lines are showing up clearly on the Mercury Mount which indicates she has natural healing abilities and she'll take up a path in the healing field.

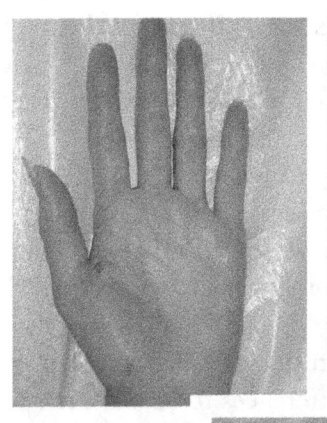

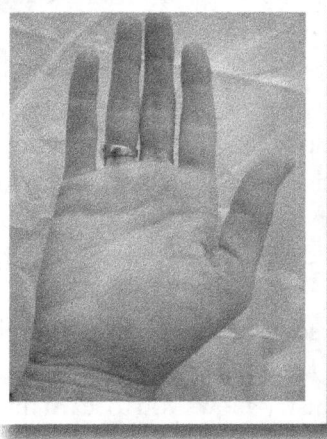

In Conclusion

Palmistry can help us discover just how compatible we are with a current or potential partner. Besides revealing your inner nature, your hands can also show you what to expect in love. If you let them 'speak', the hands provide you with many clues as to whether – and when – you and a possible partner might be suited for a satisfying relationship.

Most marriage counselors and relationship experts agree, that a successful long-term relationship is generally the result of shared interests and similar personality traits. This is not to say that we should mirror our partners totally. Ideally both people should have similar attitudes to issues of importance, while allowing for differences to enable each partner to learn from the other.

Sexual, emotional and psychological compatibility will provide a firm foundation for any lasting relationship. Two people with, say, inflexible square hands and fingers would obviously be very efficient partners at work, but their sexual and emotional lives would be lacking life and energy. So the lesson of love is to find a partner with whom you share a high degree of compatibility on all three levels.

The road of your life is mapped out on your palm. Palmistry allows you to learn things about yourself and others so you can take shortcuts, avoiding negative patterns and building more meaningful relationships along your journey of love.

Corinthians 1:13

If I speak in tongues of men and of angels, but have not love, I am only a resounding gong of a clanging cymbal.

If I have the gift of prophecy and can fathom all mysteries and all knowledge, and if I have a faith that can move mountains, but have not love, I am nothing. If I give all I possess to the poor and surrender my body to the flames, but have not love, I gain nothing.

Love is patient, love is kind. It does not envy, it does not boast, it is not proud.

It is not rude, it is not self seeking, it is not easily angered. It keeps no record of wrongs.

Love does not delight in evil but rejoices with the truth.

It always protects, always trusts, always hopes, always preserves.

Love never fails. But where there is prophecies, they will cease; where there are tongues,
they will be stilled; where there is knowledge, it will pass away. For we know in part and we prophesy

in part, but when perfection comes, the imperfect disappears.

When I was a child, I thought like a child, I reasoned like a child. When I became a man, I put childish ways behind me. Now we see but a poor reflection as in a mirror, then we shall see face to face.

Now I know in part, then I shall fully, even as I am fully known.

And now these three remain; Faith, Hope and Love.

But the greatest of these is LOVE.

About the Author

Max Coppa is Australia's leading expert in Palmistry, Numerology & Dream Interpretation with over 35 years experience. With an extensive background in media, Max has appeared on national television & radio, has contributed to many leading Australian magazines and is the published author of four books.

Max writes a weekly column for *That's Life Magazine* and appears on Channel 7's *The Morning Show*. Max's inspiring and practical approach brings palmistry and numerology into the 21st century and makes it accessible to all while allowing it to be quicker and 'friendlier' than most other styles.

Max is passionate about his work, and dedicated

to reading, counselling and teaching people of all ages to help them have a more fulfilling life.

> For more information about Max Coppa and
> the services he provides please visit:
> **www.maxcoppa.com**

Products and Services

Psychic Readings
In person ~ Telephone ~ Skype ~ Email by appointment only.

Workshops
Max's highly acclaimed palmistry and numerology workshops are tailored to suit the absolute beginner through to the advanced professional. Workshops are conducted throughout Australia.

Books by Max Coppa
merology – Working With Numbers
Your Love Life Add Up?
Between The Lines
odes

Monthly e-newsletter
ll of psychic guidance, special offers & s, insights into palmistry, numerology & pretation, celebrity profiles, moon phases pre.

w at www.maxcoppa.com

Connect with Max
www.facebook.com/maxcoppapsychic
www.twitter.com/maxcoppa

Learn more about Max Coppa at
www.maxcoppa.com

www.ingramcontent.com/pod-product-compliance
Lightning Source LLC
Chambersburg PA
CBHW050602300426
44112CB00013B/2028